Fun With Needlepoint

Books by Hope Hanley

Needlepoint
New Methods in Needlepoint
Needlepoint in America
Needlepoint Rugs
Fun With Needlepoint

FUN WITH NEEDLEPOINT

Hope Hanley

Photographs by Bob Burchette
Drawings by Evelyn Baird

CHARLES SCRIBNER'S SONS   NEW YORK

The green paperweight on color page 3 was worked by
Denise Heroux. Third graders of The Hill School, Middleburg,
Virginia, under the direction of Mrs. Brenda Moakler, worked
the pictures for *The Wind in the Willows* wall hanging on color
page 4, also on jacket back. The canvases are mounted
on black velvet.

Dedicated to
my market researcher,
Lee

Contents

PART I

PART II

Color photographs of the finished articles
between pages 32 and 33

Fun With Needlepoint

Needlepoint is embroidery worked on an evenly woven material called canvas. Each crossing of the canvas threads is covered with a diagonal stitch called the half cross stitch. Colonial girls called it tent stitch. Nineteenth century girls knew it as Berlin work because the patterns and wool came from Germany. Now we call it needlepoint. In England needlepoint is known as canvas work.

9

CANVAS

There are three kinds of needlepoint canvas. This is mono canvas. Mono means one. You see it is a simple single thread weave. The half cross stitch covers the crossing of two threads. The canvas may be white, tan or pinkish tan. It may have from ten to twenty-four threads per inch. This is the way canvas size is measured, by threads or "mesh" per inch.

This is penelope canvas. It is a double thread weave. The half cross stitch covers the crossing of four threads. Sometimes the double warp ↑ threads are closer together than the double weft → threads. Penelope canvas comes in white and tan from five mesh per inch to twelve mesh. The two threads make up one mesh or one set of mesh. You can separate the two threads and use the canvas as a mono canvas if you want. Canvas is usually made of sized or starched cotton.

This is leno canvas. It is a combination of mono canvas and penelope canvas. It looks like mono canvas but is woven with double threads in a special way. The warp threads are twisted between each weft thread. It comes in many sizes in white and natural. It works well for bargello.

Always buy clean canvas free from knots. Needlepoint may also be worked on nylon screening, buckram, burlap or warp cloth. The weave should be open and even.

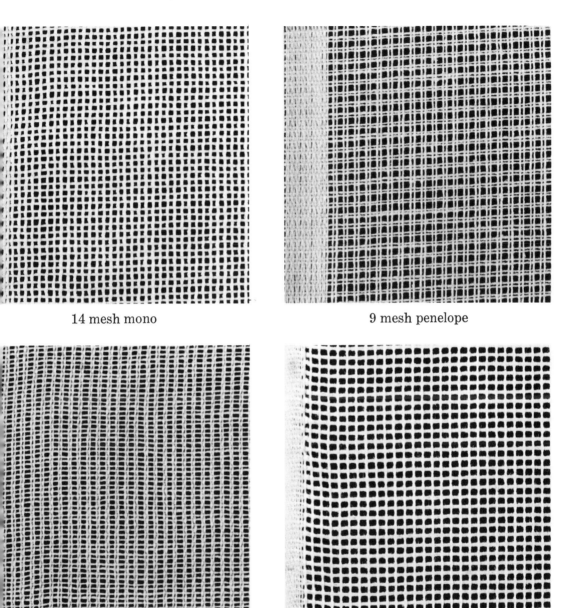

14 mesh mono

9 mesh penelope

10 mesh penelope

10 mesh leno

WOOLS

These are needlepoint wools. This one is called Persian yarn. You may use the whole strand or just one or two threads of the strand. It will fit almost any canvas.

This is tapestry wool. It works well on ten or twelve mesh canvases.

This is crewel wool, it is also used for crewel embroidery. It may be used on the very fine canvases.

This is rug wool. It is so fat that it fits only the large mesh canvases, seven mesh or less.

Cotton embroidery floss may be used for needlepoint too. You may use knitting wool, crochet perle or rafia. For durability, long fibered wools made just for needlepoint are the best.

HOW TO TELL WHAT WOOL TO USE WITH WHAT CANVAS

The way to tell if a wool fits the canvas is to work a little sample. Use the stitch you plan to use in your project. The wool should cover the canvas completely, not a speck of canvas should show through. If the wool pushes the mesh out of line, then the wool is too big for the canvas.

THREADING THE NEEDLE

Needles may be bought from size 14 to size 26. The higher the size needle, the higher the number of mesh canvas on which it will be used. Experiment. Put a needle threaded with the wool you plan to use through the canvas a few times. If the mesh are spread apart by the needle's passage, choose a finer needle.

To thread the needle, fold an inch or so of the wool back, like this. Press the fold up against the eye of the needle. Pull on the fold with your finger nails as it pops through the eye. Never wet the tip of the wool with your mouth. It makes the wool harder to thread and leaves you with a fuzzy mouth.

Each needleful of thread should be no longer than eighteen inches. If it is longer the stitches made by the end of the thread will be thinner than those at the beginning. This is caused by some of the fibers wearing off as the thread is worked.

Twirl the needle in your fingers every so often as you work. This will keep the wool from becoming too tightly twisted.

STARTING A THREAD

Start each thread this way. Put the needle in the canvas about an inch from where you want to start your first stitch. Let a little tail of wool hang out on the front of the canvas. Work your first stitches over this area. Your stitches will catch up and cover that inch of wool on the back of the canvas. When your stitches come to the "tail" pull it through to the back and snip it off close with

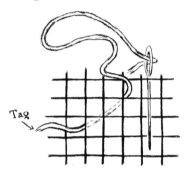

your scissors. It is important to keep the tails trimmed down so that they won't work their way to the front of the canvas.

You finish a thread off in almost the same way. When you have worked close to the end of a thread, bring the needle out about an inch from the oncoming stitches. Again let a short "tail" hang out on the front of the canvas. Try to catch up that thread with your following stitches as you work with a new needleful. Snip the tail close when you come to it.

If you have no more stitching to do, or are switching colors, finish this way. Run your needle through the backs of nearby stitches of the same color for about an inch. Snip the thread off close to the canvas.

This is the half cross stitch. It is the main needlepoint stitch. It is called half cross because it makes only half an X. Here are three ways of working it.

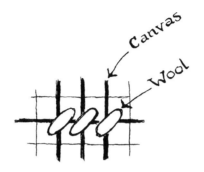

QUICK POINT—Use the quick point on penelope canvas only. It will not stay put on mono canvas.

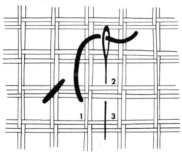

BASKET WEAVE—Use the basket weave whenever you can. It will not pull the canvas out of shape as much as the other two.

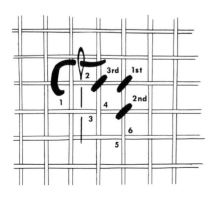
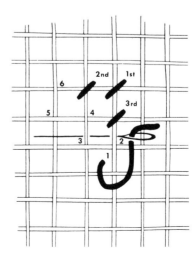

CONTINENTAL—Use the continental stitch for small areas only. Use in places where there is not room to do the basket weave, and for straight lines. Use it if you are working a graphed design.

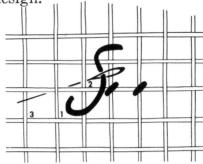

How to work the continental stitch and the basket weave stitch left-handed:

To work the continental stitch left-handed, simply turn the diagram upside down and work from left to right. The stitches will slant from bottom left to upper right.

The basket weave stitch is worked from the lower left of the canvas for left-handed people. Right-handed people work it from the upper right-hand corner. Turn the diagram upside down as you did with the continental stitch.

DESIGN

It is really more fun to design your own needlepoint than it is to work over someone else's design. You can draw your own favorite things and use your own favorite colors. Make your design as fancy or as simple as you like. Fill the canvas with one big design or use a small one over and over. Do the background in one color or in stripes or squares of many colors.

Copy a design or picture from a book or magazine. Cut out shapes from colored paper and move them about until you like the way they go together. Then glue them down just where they are and use that as your design.

Simple designs with no shading look very well in needlepoint. If you want to shade use a tone darker on the outside edges of your subject. Try to keep details to a minimum. Simplify as much as you can.

If your design needs enlarging, a photographer will photostat it any size you want. You can enlarge it yourself. Trace your picture or work directly over your own drawing. Rule squares on it. Rule larger squares on a blank sheet of paper. Then square by square redraw the design.

Drawing thin diagonal lines in needlepoint can be tricky. Because the half cross stitches are slanted, a dot-dot-dot effect is the result in one direction. If you are right-handed a line from bottom right to left will dot-dot. If you are left-handed a line from bottom left to right will dot-dot. The best remedy for this is to work complete cross stitches on these lines instead of the half cross stitch. Just make sure the top stitch slants in the same direction as the rest of the half cross stitches.

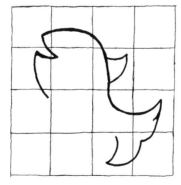

dot-dot-dot effect

COLOR

Choosing the colors for your design is a simple matter. Remember that warm bright colors attract the eye; cool colors recede. This means that the most important thing in your design should be an eye-attracting color. Contrast will achieve the same effect, a very bright color right next to a very dark color will focus attention.

The easiest way to choose your color scheme is to use your own favorite colors. If you need more colors use other shades of these colors. Artists like to use one or two colors twice in the same picture, possibly lightening or darkening the hue. This is a good practice to follow in design.

For a more balanced look a color wheel will help. You will probably want two or three main colors. Here are three ways of choosing them.

Choose a monochromatic scheme, two or three shades of the same color.

Choose an analogous scheme, colors which lie side by side on the color wheel.

Choose a complementary scheme, colors which lie opposite each other on the color wheel.

Brown is not considered a pure color, therefore it is not on the color wheel. It is a shade produced by mixing a pure color with black. Orange and black = brown. Brown will go with all colors except violet.

Grey is not on the wheel for a similar reason. It is produced by mixing black and white. Black and white are considered neutrals. They will go with any scheme.

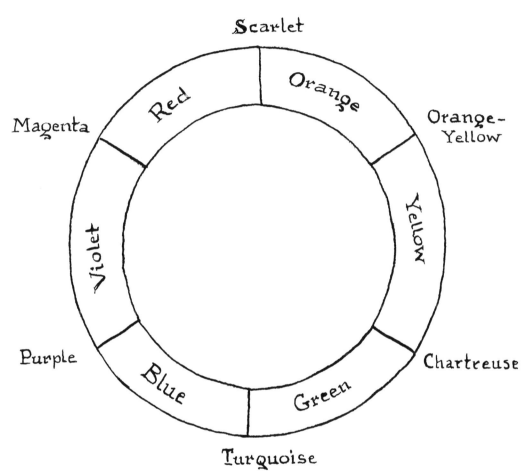

Scarlet

Orange

Orange-Yellow

Red

Magenta

Yellow

Violet

Chartreuse

Purple

Green

Blue

Turquoise

Black
White

Grey
Brown

PREPARING THE CANVAS

Before you apply the design to the canvas, the canvas must be prepared. Canvas is cut evenly along one line of mesh. Allow for a border of one and one half inches on all sides outside of your design. This canvas will not be wasted. You will need it for blocking and for putting your canvas in its finished form.

There are two ways of treating the raw edges of the cut canvas to prevent ravelling. Masking tape can be folded over the cut edge, but it doesn't always stay put. The best way is the most tiresome to do, sewing binding tape over the edges, either by hand or machine. Liquid latex may be painted on the edges; it takes about six hours to dry. RUG-STA is a good brand for this purpose; buy the bottle with the brush on it, not the spray kind.

The selvedge (the closely woven strip right on the edges) should be on the sides of your work, not on the top or bottom. Canvas "counts" from selvedge to selvedge. That is, if the canvas is supposed to be fourteen mesh, it should count that way from selvedge to selvedge. The count in the other direction may be quite different, perhaps thirteen or fifteen. This is why some finished designs look longer or shorter if you used a graph design.

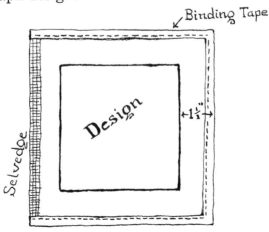

APPLYING THE DESIGN

One way to design needlepoint is on graph paper. Ten squares to the inch is a good size to use. Each SQUARE represents a STITCH.

For practice draw an apple on the graph paper, then square it out using these rules. If the line goes through the square so that more than half of the square falls on the apple side, give that square to the apple. If more than half the square falls on the background side, give that square to the background.

In order to get the design from the paper to the canvas, you must count squares, then work that many stitches on the canvas. Count, then stitch. Use the continental form of the half cross stitch for this.

Designing on graph paper is a good method for small simple designs. It is easy to get mixed up on your counting if used on large designs. To help count even a small project, cross thread your canvas. Baste a cotton thread straight across the center of your canvas, then baste another straight up from bottom to top. Draw a pencil line across and up your design on paper. Then you count so many squares from the center line on the design. Work the corresponding number of stitches from the center thread. Always start working a graph design from the center.

The other way to design needlepoint is to apply the colors directly on the canvas with crayon or paint. Crayons work very well for large undetailed designs. Any type of wax crayon will do. The idea in this method is to trace the design on to the canvas. Your original design must first be outlined with a felt-tipped pen. This is so that you will be able to see the design through the canvas. Draw an outside border on

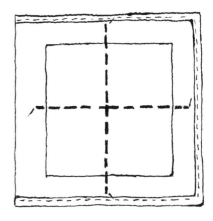

your design with the felt pen. With a crayon or chalk draw the outside border on the canvas. Lay the canvas on top of the design on a drawing board. Line up the design border with the lines drawn on the canvas and tack them straight and true to the drawing board with thumb tacks.

The design should show through the canvas enough so that you can trace it with your crayons easily. Color in solidly or just trace the outlines. Color each crossing of threads one color only. This is important. When you stitch, you should know precisely what color to use on each crossing. The test of a well-painted or colored canvas is if you can tell at a glance exactly what color each stitch should be.

Before you start to stitch over your crayoned canvas, you should remove any excess wax. Lay the canvas out on paper towels, lay more towels on top. Go over your paper towel "sandwich" very lightly with a warm iron. Remove the towels and you are ready to stitch. Work the light colors first and the darkest ones last. This will keep the light colors free of dark fibers which come loose from the wool.

Painting the canvas with acrylic or oil paints is another way of applying the design. Paints are indicated when your design is large but has many small details, or if the design is very small. Again the canvas is tacked over the felt-tipped pen outlined design. The sides must be lined up as with the crayoned canvas.

Of the two mediums, acrylic paints and oil paint, the acrylics are to be preferred. They mix with water, and the brushes can be cleaned with water. There is no fire hazard. They dry within a few hours. Oil paints must be thinned with turpentine, and the brushes cleaned with turpentine. A few drops of Japan dryer must be added to each color to hasten the drying time. Japan dryer is flammable. The drying time for oils is at least twenty-four hours.

The consistency of the paint should be the same for both mediums. It should be as thick as cream. If the paint clogs the mesh it is too thick. If it soaks through to the paper it is too thin. Use a fine brush to paint your design. Most designers do not bother to paint in the background color.

If you have some clear plastic spray or Liquitex Gloss Polymer Medium, use it over your design when the paint is quite dry. This will give the canvas a more professional look. It will also protect the paint from running if cleaning fluid is ever used on it in its future life. The canvas may be stitched over in a few hours after this treatment.

Only certain brands of magic markers are safe to use. To find out if yours are safe, mark a scrap of canvas with all the colors you mean to use. Wet the canvas and lay a paper towel over it. Wait an hour, then check to see if any color has come off on the paper towel. The danger is that color will run not only in its own area, but in the color next to it. If your project is wet blocked, or ever dry cleaned, it could be ruined by the running colors. Please test before using magic markers. Never use water colors, poster paints or colored pencils. They will all run.

BLOCKING

When you have finished stitching your project, it should be blocked to give it that shop-fresh look. Do this before you frame, use the binding-stitch, or put on any finishing touches. If your needlepoint is not out of shape from stitching, or if only slightly out of shape, a pressing should do the trick. Put the work face down on the ironing board and put a damp cloth over it. Press it lightly with a hot iron. If it needs straightening, tug here and there. Press again.

If the needlepoint needs more straightening, roll it up in a wet towel or sheet. Put this bundle in a plastic bag for six to twenty-four hours. You will need a clean board and some aluminum tacks for the next step (aluminum will not rust). Cover the board with brown paper. Lay your project face down on the paper. Pull and tug on the canvas until it seems straight and true on all sides.

Tack the work to the board, starting in the center of all four sides. Place your tacks about a half inch out from the finished stitches. Tack all the corners, then fill in in between. The canvas should be fairly taut. When the canvas dries, the sizing should have rearranged itself so that the canvas will stay the way you want it. It should take about twenty-four hours to dry.

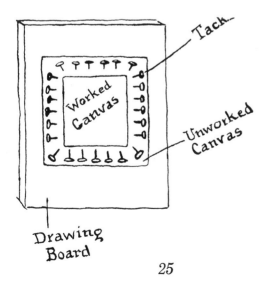

If the project is very much out of shape you will have to wet the canvas thoroughly in the sink. Do not soak it. Roll the needlepoint in a towel. Squeeze the roll to remove the excess water. Tug and pull on the canvas to make it straight. Lay it out on a brown-paper-covered board and start tacking. You may have to tug and pull some more as you tack. Canvas treated this way takes longer to dry.

Some people like to wash their work before blocking. Now is the time. Use a very mild soap. Do not soak the needlepoint. Only wash or wet needlepoint if you are *sure* that the paint used will not run.

ESTIMATING WOOL

This is how you figure how much wool you will need. Measure off four 18 inch strands of the wool you plan to use. Work an inch square sample on the canvas you plan to use in the stitch you plan to use. When you have finished measure any wool that you have left in your needle and add that amount to any strands you have left over. Subtract that amount from the total of the strands (72 inches). The result is the square inchage.

Now measure the length and width of the area you wish to cover. You may have to guess estimate sometimes. Multiply the length by the width in inches. Multiply this answer by the square inchage figure. Divide the result by 36 to get your yardage. This must be done for each color, unless you can guess estimate that something will only require a few strands. It is better to buy too much wool than too little. Many shops figure that one strand of Persian yarn will cover one square inch of ten mesh canvas, two threads of one strand will cover one square inch of fourteen mesh canvas, all worked in half cross stitch. One strand of Persian usually measures about one yard and a half. This is a generous estimate.

Fun With Needlepoint

PART II

Following are fifteen needlepoint projects. The first few are very simple, the rest are more complicated. Several different stitches are shown, several ways of finishing projects are included. A list before each project will tell you all of the things you will need. Certain things, such as embroidery frames, are not absolutley necessary, but will make the job easier. Happy Stitching!

A Felt-Framed
Pincushion

*Canvas and wool
sewing thread
felt
cotton for stuffing*

This is a good project on which to try graph paper designing and the quick point stitch. The needle-point panel itself need only be about three inches by four. Allow the usual finishing border of at least an inch and a half on all sides. Cut the canvas and treat the cut edges so they will not ravel. (Binding tape, masking tape or latex.)

In the working area of your canvas, count out in each direction how many mesh you will have to work with. Count out the same number of squares on the graph paper. Make your design fit into this area.

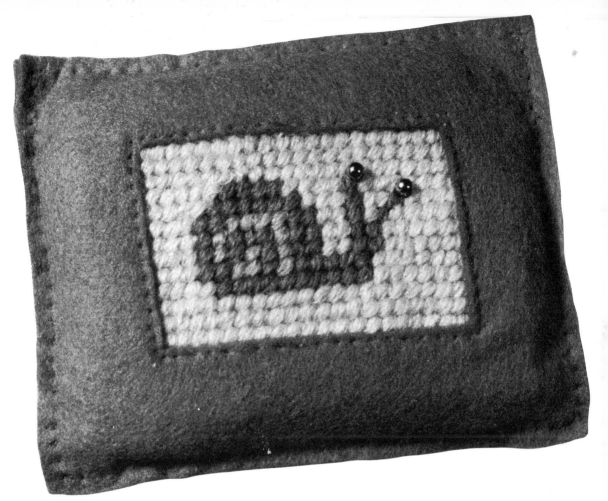

7 mesh penelope

Find the center of your design and your canvas, and work the needlepoint. If your design is a creature with a bead for an eye, leave that one eye mesh bare of stitches.

When the stitching is completed, your needlepoint should be blocked. Probably all it will need is a damp cloth pressing. Let the canvas dry for an hour and then sew the bead into the eye mesh. Sew it on with sewing thread and a half cross stitch. Secure the thread firmly on the back of the canvas.

Measure the finished needlepoint in both directions. To each measurement add three or four inches. This will give you an ample felt border. Cut two pieces to these measurements. Use embroidery scissors to cut a window in one of the pieces. Cut it to the exact measurement of the needlepoint. A piece of chalk will mark lines on felt. It will brush off easily.

Trim away the canvas border at least three-quarters of an inch from the needlepoint. Pin the needlepoint into place in the felt window. Sew it with tiny stitches using thread the same color as the felt. Sew the two pieces of felt together right sides out. Sew them on three sides leaving one open for the cotton stuffing. Stuff the corners first. Use the handle of a spoon to poke the cotton back into the corners. When it is stuffed, sew up the fourth side. Now you are finished!

A Coaster

Canvas and wool
sheet cork (or felt)
glue
cotton thread

The coaster will give you a chance to try out the basket weave stitch. A new stitch is presented, the double cross stitch. If your design is simple, it could be applied to the canvas with crayons.

Coasters are usually about three and a half inches each way. They could be larger or smaller. The big cross in the double cross stitch covers four mesh each way. This means that the space devoted to the stitch must be counted out. You must be able to divide the alloted total of mesh by four.

Cut the canvas with the usual finishing border of at least one and a half. Bind or treat the cut edges to prevent ravelling.

18 mesh mono

Work the large cross stitches first. Be sure that all the stitches cross in the same direction. Work the little upright cross stitches in the spaces left. Fill the background out with basket weave stitch.

A simple steam pressing should be all the blocking that your coaster will need. Trim away the unworked canvas to within three-quarters of an inch of the work. Fold in the tip of each corner as far as the needlepoint. Do this corner by corner with the canvas wrong side up. Fold back the sides right along the edge of the needlepoint. With sewing thread baste over each corner to hold them down. This is called mitering the corners. No bare canvas should show when you turn the canvas right side up.

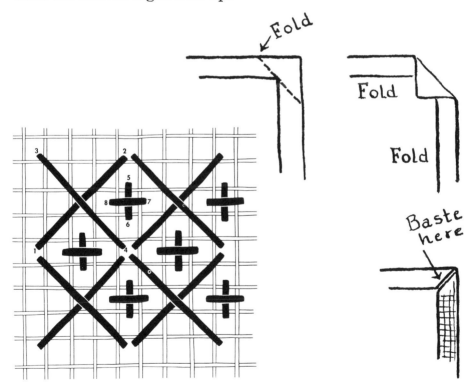

Put the needlepoint on top of your cork or felt sheet. Cut the sheet so that it is just a scant eighth of an inch larger than the needlepoint. Cover the felt or cork with glue. RUG-STA, a liquid latex obtainable by the jar at the hardware store, or ELMER'S GLUE will work very well. Cover the felt or cork almost to the edge. Set the needlepoint firmly in place. You may want to put a stack of magazines on it to make sure it sticks evenly. Let it dry three or four hours. Now you are finished.

A Needlebook

Canvas and wool
felt
thread
liquid latex (RUG-STA) or
  white nail polish
paints

The hippopotamus on the pictured needlebook was painted on the canvas. Why don't you try painting your design on your needlebook? You can use the continental stitch for the details. The edges of the needlebook will be covered with a crewel stitch, the buttonhole stitch.

The needlecase may be any size you want it to be. Just make sure that you have the same number of mesh on the front cover as on the back. Then the covers will be even. Two mesh should be left bare right in the middle of the case for the fold. Three mesh should be saved around all the outside edges. Over these mesh you will later work the buttonhole stitch.

needlecase unfolded, showing
front and back

14 mesh mono

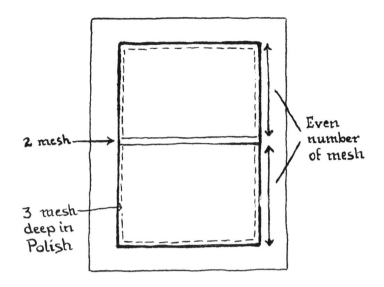

2 mesh —→

Even number of mesh

3 mesh deep in Polish

Paint these three mesh now with liquid latex or white nail polish. Be very neat and try not to go into the design area. Even though you have just prepared one outside edge, while you are working your stitches and blocking the canvas you will need the usual inch and a half border. Cut the canvas and bind or treat the edges to prevent ravelling.

Paint your design, following suggestions in the first part of the book. Work the needlepoint. The continental stitch is just for the small small areas, and the one line details. Use the basket weave stitch wherever you can. When you have finished stitching, block your canvas. When it is dry trim away the finishing border. Cut just along your latexed three mesh border.

Work the buttonhole stitch around the latexed border. Fasten your beginning and ending threads in the backs of nearby stitches. You may need an extra strand of wool for the buttonhole edging to make it cover properly. Don't work

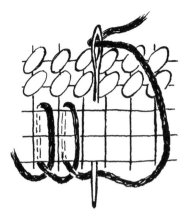

the stitch too tightly. You want it to stand out from the canvas, not curl under. When you come to a corner, keep using the same corner mesh over and over until you have covered the corner with stitches.

Cut a piece of felt for the lining. It should be an eighth of an inch smaller on the longer sides and a quarter of inch smaller at the short ends. This shortness will help it to fit when the case is folded and closed. Using cotton thread, neatly stitch the lining into place.

needlecase
folded

40

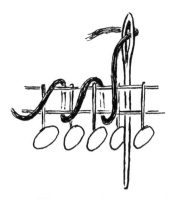

The two bare mesh left in the middle of the case will be covered with a whip stitch. Again you will probably need an extra strand of wool to cover the canvas completely. Fasten your beginning and ending threads in the back of nearby stitches. Fold the needlebook in half along the line of bare mesh to work the whip stitch. This stitch is supposed to help keep the fold. It may pick up some of the felt lining, this is all right.

With a damp cloth and hot iron, press the folded case flat. Now you are finished!

A Car Pillow

Canvas and wool
pillow backing of cloth or felt
old stockings or other stuffing
cotton thread
2 finishing nails
a child's wooden block

Anyone riding in a bucket-seated car for any length of time knows about that hollow place at the small of your back. This little pillow was designed to just fill that hollow. Make one for your parents' car. After they try it you will soon have orders for more. On the pillow pictured you can see how a single line of stitches from bottom right to upper left was curved. The complete cross stitch links the dot-dot-dot stitches together. (See page 17 of the first section of this book.) A simple cording has been stitched to the edge of the pillow. It gives the knife edge a more finished look.

10 mesh mono

The pillow shown is ten inches square. You might like to make yours a rectangle, perhaps eight by ten inches. Make sure you have the usual inch and a half finishing border. Bind or treat the edges so that they will not ravel. Design your canvas as you will. A series of colored stripes worked in the basket weave stitch is very masculine looking. A small "kit" bought from the needlework shop could be used.

When your stitching is finished, block the canvas. Measure the finished work. Cut the pillow backing to fit with three quarters of an inch extra on all sides. Lay the canvas and the backing material down face to face. Baste the pieces together. Leave a four inch gap in the basting for later stuffing.

If you have a sewing machine, use it for the next step. Otherwise the job will have to be done by hand. With the canvas side up, machine stitch down the middle of the last row of needlepoint stitches. Sew as straight a seam as you can. If sewn by hand, work as closely as possible to the last row of needlepoint stitches. Don't forget to leave that four inch space open for stuffing!

Trim the finishing border canvas away to within three-quarters of an inch from the work. Trim a trifle closer at the corners. Turn the canvas right side out. Poke into the corners with a spoon handle to make them point out. Stuff the pillow with old nylon stockings. (If panti-hose are used, please cut off the elastic waistband first.) Hand stitch the stuffing opening, but leave one inch still open for the cording ends. With a damp cloth and a hot iron, smarten up the edges of the pillow and the corners.

To make the cording you will need to make a cording

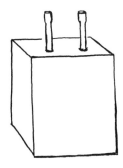

machine. It is called a lucet. You will need two "finishing" nails. They do not have a flat head, just a slight bulge at the top. You will also need a child's wooden building block. Any other piece of hard wood of the same shape or size will do as well. Drive the finishing nails into one end of the block, one inch apart and a quarter of an inch in.

You will need approximately eight yards of wool to make the cording. You may need more if your pillow is larger than ten by ten inches. The wool must be in one long piece. Persian wool is available in some shops in little skeins. About a quarter of a skein of tapestry yarn will be enough.

Tie a small noose in the end of the yarn. Loop the noose over one of the nails. Hold the end of the noose knot against the block and wrap the working thread around each nail. On the nail with two loops, take the bottom loop and pull it

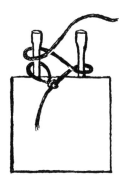

off the nail. Pull the working thread so that the cording is pulled tight and into the center between the two nails. Continue wrapping the working thread around first one nail and then the other, always pulling the bottom thread up and off the nail. Continue pulling on the working thread to keep the cording tight and in the center. Make enough cording to go around the pillow plus an inch to spare. Finish off by cutting the working thread and then threading it through the two remaining loops. Pull them off the nails and pull the working thread tight.

What you have made is a knitted cording. Put one end of it in the inch space between the backing and the canvas. Blind stitch it to the last row of needlepoint stitches with sewing thread. When you come around to the inch space again, tuck the end of the cording inside. Cross the end of the cording over the beginning and stitch them together. This will make the cording look more continuous. Close up the inch space. Now you are finished!

A Doll House Rug

Canvas and wool
sewing thread
an embroidery frame perhaps

A doll house rug must be very thin so that it will not tilt the dolls' furniture too much. Therefore a very thin canvas must be used for a dolls' needlepoint rug. Cross stitch canvas with a blue thread every ten rows of mesh is the best kind to use. The rug is one of the easiest projects in this book. Besides the actual stitching all you have to do is to make a little hem on two sides of the canvas. The stitching is worked right through the hems. A binding stitch is worked over the fold and the other two sides are ravelled. If your rug is large you may want to use a frame. This will keep the canvas from slanting sideways, the rug will always lie true and straight.

11 mesh cross stitch canvas

Designing for rugs is a little different than most designing. You have to remember to keep the design in scale. For instance, a very large cat with a checkered background would be an overpowering design for a dolls' living room. It would like an old pillow cover or picture mislaid on the floor. Many small cats on a plain background would be more in scale.

A border will really improve any rug design. Just one or two lines around the edge will do. Try to include a color in the border or the design that is already present in the furnishings. This will make the rug look more as if it really belonged in that room.

Cross stitch canvas is the best canvas to use because it is so thin. The blue threads should run parallel to the short end of the rug. You will ravel them out when you make the fringe for the rug.

To prepare the canvas for working, include a half inch border on the long sides and the usual inch and half on the ends. Fold along one set of mesh the half inch borders on the long sides. Baste them to the back of the canvas or machine stitch if you have a sewing machine. Treat or bind the short sides of the canvas, including the fold-back, to prevent ravelling. You will be working right through the folded back canvas. Match mesh on top of mesh so that it looks as if there were just one layer of canvas there. Do not work over the row of mesh on which you folded. That will be covered later with the finishing stitch.

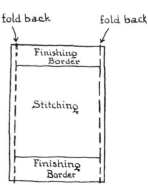

49

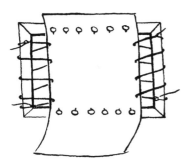

Apply your design. If the rug is large—eight by ten inches would be considered large in doll house circles—now is the time to put it into the embroidery frame. An old picture frame will do if you don't want to buy a stretcher frame. Tack one end right to the frame through the finishing border. If the picture frame is too small you will have to tack through the working canvas. Make sure your thumb tacks do not split the thread of the canvas but go into the spaces instead. Using sewing thread and a needle, lash the sides of the rug to the frame. Pick up the fold mesh, do not go into the working area. Tie the thread securely. When you have finished working the area in the frame, cut the lashing threads, remove the thumb tacks and move the canvas so that unworked canvas is presented. Then re-tack, and re-lash.

A stretcher frame works pretty much the same way. The only difference is that you can turn your canvas like a scroll on the long stretchers. The canvas may be basted to the tapes fastened to the stretchers instead of tacked. Tighten the screws to make the canvas nice and taut. You will be using two hands to work with a frame. One hand to punch the needle into the canvas and the other underneath to receive the needle and send it back up to the surface. You will find that using a frame will make your stitches look very even.

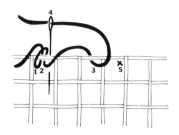

Whether you used a frame or not, your rug will still need a little touch-up pressing. If your unframed rug needs a major blocking, put the tacks into the finishing border and not into the sides.

The binding stitch is worked along the set of folded mesh at the sides. Turn the canvas face down and run the wool along the backs of nearby stitches to fasten it. Take the needle over the edge of the canvas and bring it towards you through the very first mesh. The needle is always pointing toward you with the binding stitch. Now follow the diagram. Always when going forward put your needle in the next empty mesh. Always when going back skip one mesh. When you finish a thread run it into the backs of nearby stitches. Start the next thread the same way, and pick up exactly where you left off.

When you have come to the end of the row, stop going forward a mesh. Just keep working the same forward mesh until the backward stitches catch up. This will bring the stitch to a neat finish. Work the binding stitch on both sides of the rug.

Trim off the finishing border about three quarters of an inch from the needlework. Ravel the canvas right up to the needlework. Pull one thread at a time, otherwise they will tangle. Now you are finished.

The Comb Case

Canvas and wool
sewing thread
seam binding or grosgrain
ribbon
a piece of Velcro or a large
snap
a comb

The comb case can grow into a ruler or yardstick case if you are very ambitious. All you need is more canvas. The binding stitch is used again, this time as an edging and to join two pieces of canvas.

The canvas you use should be a fairly light and soft one. Heavy white mono-canvas is not suitable, it makes too fat a case.

The first thing you need is the comb for which you are making the case. Measure the comb, its length and width. To the length you must add four inches. This will allow for the flap and any taking up that the canvas might do as it is stitched. To the width you must add an inch.

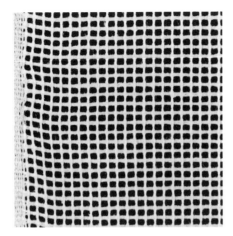

10 mesh leno

photo courtesy of Hugh Grubb

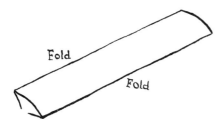

After you have figured out your design, cut your canvas. Allow for the usual finishing border of an inch and a half all the way around. Treat or bind the canvas to prevent ravelling. You may want to work the long sides of the case the way the sides of the rug were worked (page 49). If so, both long sides should have a six mesh hem folded in. The canvas should be folded on one set of mesh if penelope is used, and two mesh if mono canvas is used. Match the two layers of mesh so that they look as if they were just one layer. Baste the hems to prevent ravelling. Bind the short ends, folds and all.

Work your needlepoint, stitching through both layers of canvas on the long sides. Do not work the fold mesh, the binding stitch will cover that later. After working your stitches, block the canvas. When it is dry, trim the finishing border to within three-quarters of an inch on the flap end of the case. Fold the long sides in if you did not work through them, and trim them too. Fold the short flap canvas down so that one set or two mesh, depending on your canvas, show for the binding stitch. With tiny blind stitches sew your ribbon or binding tape lining to the flap and down about an inch and a half into the case. Sew the lining to the backs of the last row of stitches on each side.

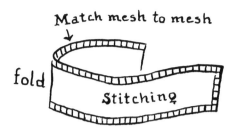

Match mesh to mesh

fold

Stitching

Fold the canvas to form the case. Start working the binding stitch, first anchoring your wool in nearby backs of stitches. Holding the sides of the case so that the fold mesh are close together, work over them as though there was only one fold of canvas there. Each mesh must have its mate, two by two, matching mesh for mesh, work up the side of the case.

To finish off a thread run it through the backs of nearby stitches. Start a new thread where the needle would have come out if you had continued on with the old thread. When joining two pieces of canvas with the binding stitch, a new thread is always started this way.

Before you reach the mouth of the case, trim the canvas at the other short end to within three quarters of an inch of the work. Fold it in so that one set of mesh or two mesh are left showing. Push the extra canvas out of the way with your needle as you work past it and on up and around the flap. Work the binding stitch around the corners just as you would the straight away, back and forth as usual.

Work the other side of the case. Work a row of binding stitch over the set of mesh left at the inside of the case. Give the case a pressing with a damp cloth and a hot iron to flatten it out. Sew the snap or velcro in place on the flap and on the body of the case. Now you are finished!

A Head Band

Canvas and wool
beads
binding tape for lining or
  grosgrain ribbon
sewing thread
elastic, half or quarter inch
  wide

The head band is a very quick thing to make because of the stitch used. It is called bargello. It covers several mesh in one long stitch so the canvas covers rapidly. Beads trim the head band to add a gay touch. Berlin work and beads were very popular in the nineteenth century.

Head bands are usually eighteen inches long. The elastic goes the rest of the way. It can be as wide as you want. Bargello may only be worked on mono-canvas. If penelope is used the two threads show right through the upright stitches. A leno canvas is all right because although it is two thread, the two threads are twisted together.

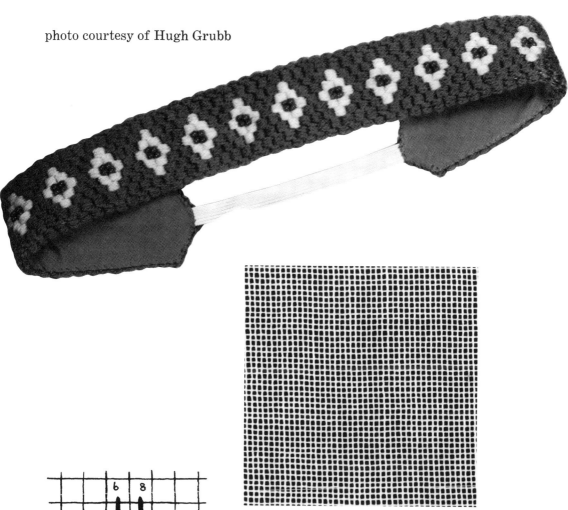

photo courtesy of Hugh Grubb

18 mesh mono

A crisp thin canvas would be best for this project. You will need more wool in your needle to cover the canvas than you do for the half cross stitch. No canvas should show through the stitches. Try out your stitches and wool on a spare piece of canvas first. The diagramed pattern may be used or you may want to work out your own. Plan to save four crossing mesh per bead as shown in the diagramed pattern.

Bargello will help your half cross stitching. It must be worked evenly and rather loosely. You will find that this eveness will carry over into the next piece of half cross stitch you do. With bargello the canvas threads should not be pulled out of place at all.

When your canvas is measured off, including the usual inch and a half finishing border, cut it and bind the edges. Binding is best because the canvas will be so narrow that latex would catch your wool too much. Fold the canvas in half lengthwise to find the center mesh. Run a cotton sewing thread along the center mesh. This will help you keep the pattern on center as you work it. You will be working from this book or your own pattern so painting will not be required.

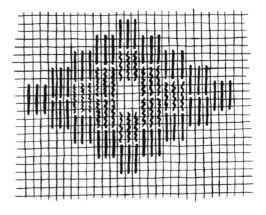

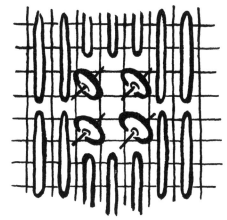

beads attached

Start stitching at the center and work out. Finish each thread by running the needle under the backs of nearby stitches for at least an inch. Trim the wool tags away so that they won't be caught up and ride another stitch to the front.

When the stitching is completed, press with a damp cloth and a hot iron with the canvas face down. Sew the beads on next. Each bead should be large enough to completely cover the four mesh alloted. Use two strands of thread in a sewing or beading needle. Secure the thread with a knot in a nearby stitch back. Do this before and after each set is attached to keep the beads firmly in place. They are sewn on with a half cross stitch, so they will sit diagonally in their place.

Trim the finishing border to within three-quarters of an inch of the work. Fold the bare canvas back and stitch it down flat with basting stitches. No bare canvas should show on the front, a little of the stitching will show on the back. Blind stitch the lining to the first bare thread of canvas next to the needlework. If your binding tape is too wide, cut it to size, fold a new hem and press it flat.

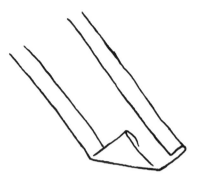

When you come to the end of one side, fold the canvas diagonally to follow the line of the stitching. Fold up the point produced by doing so. Tack that down with a few stitches. Sew one end of a four and a half piece of elastic tape to that. Sew it very securely. Cover it with lining and then continue sewing the lining up the other side. Treat the other end of the head band the same way. Press lightly on the edges. Now you are finished!

The Belt

Canvas and wool
belt buckles or clasps
ribbon or binding tape
thread

The belt looks as if it were made in bargello stitch but it isn't. It is really the long cross stitch, and works only on penelope canvas. Worked in a bargello-like pattern, it looks like the real thing unless closely examined.

Before you start your belt the buckle or clasps must be bought. This is so you will know how wide to make the belt. Measure the width of the space alloted on the buckle for the belt and then add a third of an inch for draw-up as the belt is worked. Measure the length of the buckle and subtract that from your waist measurement. Add an extra inch to take care

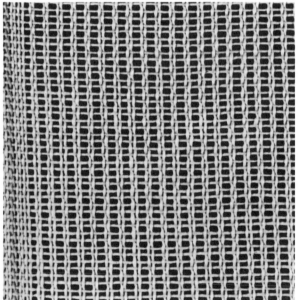

7 mesh penelope

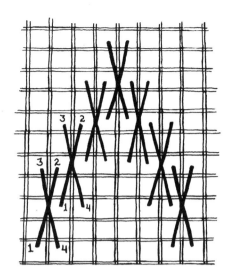

of the half inch turn back on the buckles. Use the usual inch and a half finishing border and bind the edges so that the canvas will not ravel as you work. Masking tape or latex is too snaggy for this narrow piece of work. Fold the canvas in half to find its middle, and mark it with a pin. Fold the canvas lengthwise to find the exact dead center and start your stitching there. Work towards the ends.

Complete each stitch before going on to the next. Don't make all the strokes in one direction and then come back and do all the strokes in the other direction. Completing the stitches is more economical of wool and puts much less bulk on the back of the canvas. Do make sure your stitches all cross in the same direction.

When you think you have worked enough, try the belt around your waist. Remember to include that half inch of turn-back on each end. If you have worked enough, steam press the canvas face down with a hot iron and a damp cloth.

Work the binding stitch along the mesh nearest the work. Hold the belt with the wrong side facing you as you work it.

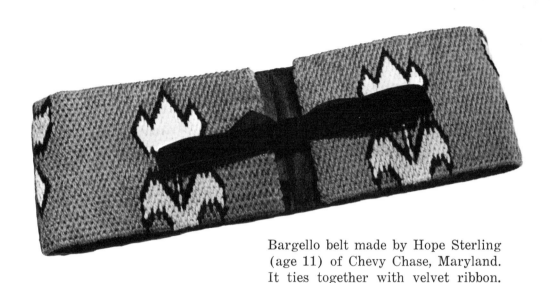

Bargello belt made by Hope Sterling (age 11) of Chevy Chase, Maryland. It ties together with velvet ribbon.

Stitch here

Use fewer strands of wool in the needle for the binding stitch unless you want a fat edging. Work both sides and press again. Fold the finishing canvas down and baste it to the back of the belt about a quarter of an inch from the binding stitch. Then trim the canvas to within a half inch of the basting.

To attach the buckles, fold the bare canvas a mesh more than the binding stitch edge. Slip the buckle on. Stitch the canvas down to the back of the belt so that the stitches will not show in the front. The half inch extra stitching should now show on the back of the belt. Stitch as firmly as you can, really lash it down. Trim the rest of the bare canvas back to within a half inch of the lashing down stitches. Attach the other buckle to the other end.

The belt may be lined with binding tape or grosgrain ribbon. If the ribbon is too wide, simply fold it back until it fits. Sew the selvedge to the belt first with tiny blind stitches. Sew the folded side next. Press again. Now you are finished!

The Camp Stool

Rug canvas and wool
aluminum camp stool
felt
carpet thread and sewing
thread

The camp stool is made very much like the belt is made. The difference is the way the canvas is attached to the stool. Four rows of mesh are left bare of stitches on each side of the canvas. These mesh are worked later along with another layer of canvas underneath. This makes a stronger joint than just stitching with thread.

First you must buy your camp stool. Sears Roebuck or any sporting goods store carry aluminum stools for just a couple of dollars. You want a folding X frame stool.

The canvas used should be rug canvas. Working this kind of join on a finer mesh canvas would be very tiresome. Make sure that the canvas that you use has no knots or weak threads.

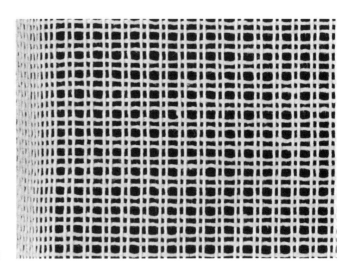

5 mesh rug canvas

To figure how much canvas will be needed measure first the circumference of the bar to which the present seat is attached. To this measurement add an inch for the join, and an inch and a half for the space the wool will take up around the bar. Double this figure (for the other side) and add it to the width of the seat already on the stool. The usual inch and a half finishing border should be included too. That takes care of the width measurements.

Now measure how long the seat is and add an inch for canvas draw-up and two inches for the fold back hems. Cut the canvas and fold the inch hems back on the long sides of the canvas. Baste them in place. Bind the short ends of the canvas or put on masking tape to prevent ravelling. You will, as usual, be working right through the fold back hems as though there was just one piece of canvas there. Rug wool is ideal for this project but if you don't have that, three full strands of Persian will work quite well.

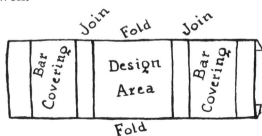

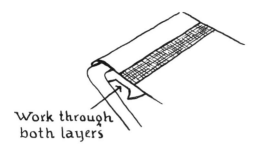
Work through
both layers

While planning your design, keep in mind the four mesh on each side saved for the join. Work your design, skip the four mesh and then work the canvas that goes around the bars. Roll the canvas like a scroll to make it easier to hold. The bar panels are a good place to add your name and the date.

When you have finished your needlework, a steam pressing may be all that will be necessary but if you must tack the canvas down on a blocking board, just tack the short ends using the finishing border.

Work the binding stitch over the folded edge from one end of the canvas to the other. Work right over the four mesh gaps in the needlework. Work the other side. Place the canvas on the stool. Match up the four mesh wide gap with the bare canvas next to the stitching underneath. Baste the layers together so that the needlepoint will be easier to work, matching mesh over mesh. Work the needlepoint stitches.

Work the other join the same way. Measure for the felt lining. It should cover the underside of the stool from right next to the binding stitch to right next to your needlepoint stitching. Trim the finishing border to within three mesh of the join. Use good quality felt for the lining. (Cheap felt pulls apart as you stitch it in place.) Stitch it to the edges of the binding stitch so that no canvas shows. Stitch it to the completed stitches on the bar. Now you are finished!

A Key Ring Fob

*Canvas and wool
key ring finding
needlenose pliers*

The following four projects all stem from the same basic idea. Each project introduces a new stitch or a new way of using one already learned. For instance, most people work the cross stitch in two trips across the canvas. A row of bottom stitches is completed in one trip, and then the top stitches are added on the return trip. This project will show a way of working a complete cross stitch in one trip in a rhythmic way.

A modified binding stitch, based on the running cross stitch, joins the sides of the key fob.

11 mesh penelope

It is important to use a very light penelope canvas to make the fob. Choose a simple motif as there are not many mesh to work. Initials might look very well. The fob is made on one piece of canvas. One mesh is used to fold on. The number of mesh on the front and the back must be the same so that they will join evenly. Two inches square is a nice size for a key chain fob. Remember the inch and a half finishing border all the way around. The motif should be worked twice, once for each side. The heart motif pictured was worked in cross stitch. Follow the diagram to work it. If you want the top stitch to follow the same direction as the half cross stitch background work it the first way. If you don't care if the top stitch slants in the opposite direction use the second diagram. The second way is less awkward to work.

top stroke slanting right to left

X

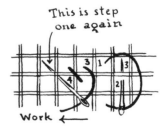

top stroke slanting left to right

X

71

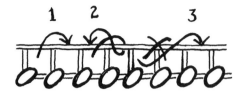

When the stitching is completed, steam press the fold with a damp cloth and a hot iron. Trim the finishing border away within six mesh of the needlework. Fold the edges in on one set of mesh right next to the stitching. Work the running cross stitch on that row of mesh. Start it on the fold and then proceed around the corners. Join the two sides by matching mesh for mesh on each side and stitching as though they were just one. The running cross stitch makes a fatter, shorter braid on the edge than does the binding stitch. To finish or start a new thread, run the needle down into the body of the stitching and leave a tag of thread sticking out which you can trim later. Start the new thread with the needle coming out where it would have been had you continued with the same thread. To work the corners just fold the canvas in and poke the extra canvas out of your way with the needle as you stitch.

When you have finished, steam press the fob once more to smarten up its corners. With the needlenose pliers open the link of the key chain to which you are going to add the fob. Open it wide enough so that it will slip over the fob. Push it in far enough so that it will pierce the canvas, not just the running cross stitch. Work the link through the canvas so that you can close it with the pliers. Now you are finished.

A Paper Weight

Canvas and wool
cotton stuffing
an old stocking or two
a dipsy fishing weight or a
  package of small shot
  weights
a hammer and pliers

The paper weight shows us a join that is very simple and that can be done in two colors if you like. It is worked in two trips around the edge of the finished canvas. The old way of working the cross stitch is used, the strokes done in one direction on one trip, and the other direction on the second trip.

Dipsy Weight

Shot
Weights

The paper weight may be any shape you like if you use the shot weights. The dipsy weight when pounded flat is round, therefore a square shape is required if you use that weight. Dipsy weights and shot weights can be bought at the

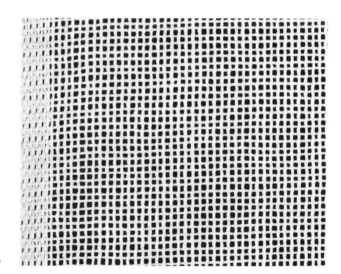

14 mesh mono

hardware store. Ask for a three ounce dipsy or bass casting weight. One or two boxes of the shot weights will be enough.

Grasp the ring of the dipsy weight with the pliers and twist back and forth until the ring breaks off. If any of the ring remains, don't worry, it will get lost in the lead when you flatten the weight. Set the weight on concrete or on a board and start to pound on it. It should be pancake shaped when you are finished, and no more than a half inch thick.

Measure your lead pancake and allow a generous half inch more canvas on all sides. The usual inch and a half finishing border should be included. The paper weight is made in one piece and folded in half as the key chain fob was made. If you use mono-canvas, save two mesh in the middle for the fold, and one set of mesh if you use penelope. Cut your canvas and treat the edges with latex or bind with binding tape or masking tape to prevent the canvas from ravelling.

Work your design. Your name and the date could go on the bottom half if you didn't want to repeat the motif. When your stitching is finished, block the canvas. Trim the finishing border to within three quarters of an inch of the work. Fold the tips of the four corners of the canvas in, folding on one set of mesh, or on two mesh depending on the canvas. Fold the sides in next on a set of mesh or two mesh. With sewing thread stitch the folded corners down with basting thread. Fold the canvas in half where it is meant to be folded. Whip the sides of the paper weight together, using the fold mesh. Before you whip the third side, the weights and the stuffing have to go in.

The shot weights may go into the foot of an old stocking to keep them from scattering. Stuff the corners of the weight

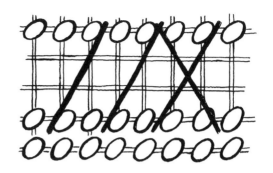

with cotton first, using the handle of a spoon to force the cotton into the corners. Put in the shot weights and finish whipping. With the dipsy weight the corners should have just a little cotton stuffed in. Then the weight should be wrapped in a stocking from which the top and the toe have been cut off. Finish whipping the third side.

The cross stitch is worked up into the completed stitching one row both top and bottom. (See the diagram) Work the stitch in two trips around the weight. Work the second trip in another color if you like. If the cross stitch does not cover the way you want it to, use another thread of wool in your needle. Now you are finished.

The Lady Bug

Canvas and wool
stuffing
thread
a pipe cleaner
a large needle

Madame lady bug brings us back to the binding stitch. This time it is used on a diagonal slant to give the lady bug her shape. Use a light penelope canvas. A heavy mono canvas is too hard to work with for such a small item.

The design may be applied with crayons. Outlines are all that is needed, you don't have to color in everything. As the two previous projects were made, the bug is made of one piece of canvas and then folded. One set of mesh should be counted for the fold. The bug is twenty-two mesh wide and twenty-

9 mesh penelope

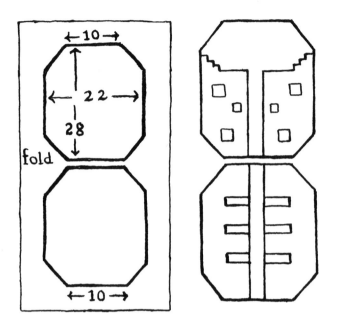

eight long. Her nose and back end are ten mesh wide. Her sides are sixteen mesh long. The diagonals are all six mesh deep. No matter what size mesh canvas you use, you can still use these figures.

Use the usual inch and a half finishing border. Treat or bind the cut edges of the canvas to prevent ravelling as you work it. Work your canvas and then block or steam press the work, whichever it needs. Trim the finishing canvas away within three quarters of an inch of the work. Fold the canvas on the bare mesh in the middle and start working the binding stitch. Work with the bottom of the bug facing up. When you come to the diagonal, tuck the canvas down inside so that one diagonal set of mesh shows on both sides. Matching mesh for mesh, join the two sides together.

It will seem as if the mesh are further apart than they are on the straight away. They are. Never mind, the binding

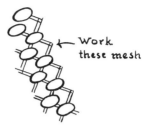

Work
these mesh

stitch will cover all. Fold the straight sides along a set of mesh on each side and continue on with the binding stitch. Work around the three corners and part way up the third side. Pause to stuff a pair of old stockings inside. Holding the sides of the bug firmly together, continue on to the end.

Thread a pipe cleaner into a large enough needle. Bend the end back so that it will stay in the needle. Run it in and out again on the bug's head where you want the antenna to be. You may need the needlenose pliers to help you grip. Cut off the bent piece of pipe cleaner. Now you are finished.

The Hedgehog

Canvas and wool
two little brown buttons
one long bead, preferably
*   black*
a crochet hook
sewing thread
cotton

The hedgehog has a lovely fuzzy back. This is formed by turkey work, a very popular stitch in the seventeenth and eighteenth centuries. He has a bead nose, shiny button eyes and tiny crocheted ears. His body is stitched in the half cross stitch worked in two different directions. This somehow gives his face more expression. It also makes it easier to work the binding stitch around his diagonal face.

The hedgehog must be worked on penelope canvas, a light one. Seven mesh per inch is ideal. Three shades of one color are needed for his body, or three colors if you like. One color goes for his body, one for his turkey work prickles, and a little of the third to make him look pricklier.

7 mesh penelope

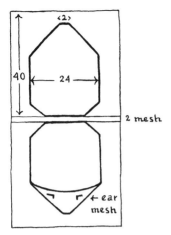

Crayons will work well to mark his outlines. You will have to do some counting out again. His body is forty mesh long on each side. One set of mesh is needed for his fold. The fold is at his bottom end. Like the fob, weight, and lady bug, he is made in one long piece. He is just twenty four mesh wide. His nose is two mesh wide, this gives eleven mesh for the diagonal part of his face on each side. His back end is fourteen mesh wide, the diagonal part is only four mesh deep.

Count thirteen mesh back from his nose and draw a line sloping two or three mesh back to the sides. Five mesh in and about three back from the diagonal line of his face draw a three mesh line for the ears. The ear mesh should be left bare, until the very last. The crocheting is the last thing to do.

The usual inch and a half finishing border should be included. Treat or bind the edges of the canvas to prevent ravelling. Start the stitching on the bottom side of the hog. It will be worked in quarters. To find the center so that it can be divided into quarters, fold the canvas first lengthwise and then width-wise. Mark the lines in with a crayon. Work the stitches on his left top quarter so that they slant towards the right. The bottom right quarter stitches should also slant to the right. The top right quarter and the bottom left quarter should slant towards the left. The face should have the left side slanting toward the right, and the right side stitches should slant towards the left. The stitches will seem to point towards the nose.

You will be surprised at the next step. The hedgehog should be blocked or steam pressed at this point. The finishing canvas should be trimmed away to within three quarters of an inch of the needlework. The turkey work will come later. It would be too hard and tangly to try to work it now, and then bind the sides.

Start the binding stitch on the fold set of mesh on his back end. Work with his bottom side facing up. Tuck the canvas inside when you come to the diagonal and work the sets of mesh nearest to the needlework, matching mesh for mesh. Work around his face and nose. Stuff his face and then his body with cotton or some other stuffing. Continue working the binding stitch back to where you started. Next comes the fuzzy stitch.

Turkey work is worked from the bottom of the area that you wish to fill up to the top. Start at the face end of the hog and work towards the tail end. It can be worked left to right or right to left. Make the loops a little more than an inch long. Use your thumb as a gauge. Do not cut them until you

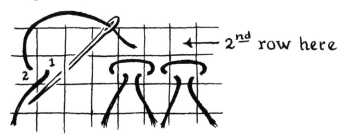

2nd row here

have finished the whole job. At random, work in a stitch of the third color, perhaps one or two a row. When you have finished, trim the loops unevenly. You don't want them to be all the same length like plush.

Hold the hog over a steaming tea kettle and the fuzz will become frizzier. Sew the buttons on for the eyes, and the long bead for the nose. Thread your needle with body color wool and run it straight through his body coming out at the ear mesh. Leave a tag of wool on the underside just hanging. It can be trimmed later. Pull the needle off the thread and take up the crochet hook. Stick the crochet hook under the first set of mesh and loop the wool over it. Pull it back out from the mesh, holding on to the wool loop with the hook. From the trailing end of the wool thread pull another loop of wool through the first one. Leaving that loop on the hook, go under another set of mesh and from the trailing end of the wool form another loop. Pull the new loop through the one left from before. Do this once more on the third set of mesh. When you are down to the last loop pull the trailing end through it. Pull tightly. Thread the trailing end in your needle and secure the ends of the ears to the face if they seem to be floppy. Then run the needle through the body of the hog and cut the wool off close to the body. Work the other ear the same way. Now you are finished.

The

See-Through Tote

Canvas and wool
sewing thread
white nail polish or base coat
plastic spray

The see through tote takes only four or five hours to make because there is no background to do. Only two stitches are used, the continental version of the half cross stitch, and a whip stitch over the folded edges of the finished tote.

You need a piece of rug canvas about nineteen inches long and eleven inches wide. Two extra pieces of canvas for handles should be a foot long and exactly ten mesh wide.

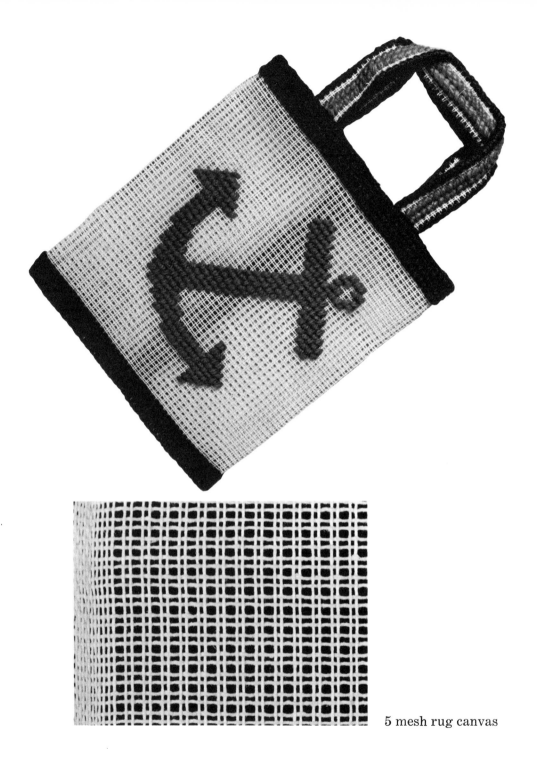

5 mesh rug canvas

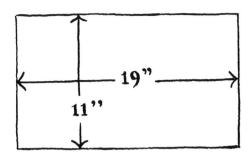

The edges of all three pieces should be painted with white nail polish or base coat. Paint carefully just the outside set of mesh. When the nail polish is dry, all three pieces should be sprayed with plastic spray. The purpose of this is to keep the unworked canvas clean. When everything is dry the stitching can begin.

Overlap one short end over the other, three mesh deep. Pin the overlap and squash the canvas flat. Now you know how many mesh you have in the front of the tote for your motif. Seven mesh at both the top and the bottom of the long sides are needed for the top hem and joining of the bottom. Since the canvas must stay clean it would be best if your designing were done on graph paper and then counted out onto the canvas.

The back of the canvas must be kept very neat as there will be no lining to cover untidy tags. Trim them closely. When the motif stitching is completed, baste the three mesh layover for the back seam. Match mesh over mesh so that it looks as though there were only one layer of canvas there. Start working the continental stitch seven mesh from the top along the layover mesh. Stop the row seven mesh short of the edge. Work the three rows, again the stitches should look just as neat inside as out.

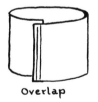

Overlap

To join the bottom, fold in the canvas on the fourth set of mesh from the edge. Match the layers of canvas so that it looks like just one layer, though actually it is four. Baste loosely to hold them in place as you work. Start working the continental stitch on the front. To give a more continuous look to the stitch on both the front and the back, start and finish your wool this way. When finishing leave the old thread in the path of the oncoming new stitches. Start the new thread in the backs of five or six of the old stitches. You will see that it will be hard to tell just where you started and where you finished.

Work three rows of the continental stitch this way. Then work the whip stitch over the exposed mesh on the fold and up the sides.

The handles should be worked next so that they may be attached. Fold the handles on the third set of mesh from the edge on each long side. The edges will not overlap. Baste the folds down. Work the continental stitch as you did on the bottom, starting and finishing the thread as suggested. Work within four mesh of the ends and just work the two rows in the center to cover the cut edges of the canvas.

Next fold the top of the tote inside on the fourth mesh from the edge. Baste all the way around. Baste the handles inside the tote, matching mesh for mesh, setting them in level with the turned-in hem. Then work the continental stitch all the way around the whole tote. Just three rows are needed, stitch in the handles as you go. Whip stitch both sides of the handles and around the top of the tote. Steam press the tote to give the handles and the sides a smart look. Now you are finished.

A Mobile

Rug canvas and rug wool
20 gauge galvanized wire
needlenose pliers
white nail polish
transparent nylon thread or
* white carpet thread*
Elmer's glue

Each piece of the mobile is one big needle-point stitch. Five new stitches are used to make the pieces. Each stitch is worked on two pieces of canvas and they are then sewed back to back. The hardest part of this project is to make the mobile balance.

Make your stitches about two inches apart on a piece of rug canvas. Follow the diagrams to work the stitches. Cut out each set of stitches very carefully, two mesh away from the stitching on all sides. As you can see, some of the shapes are octagonal. Paint the very outside row of mesh all the way

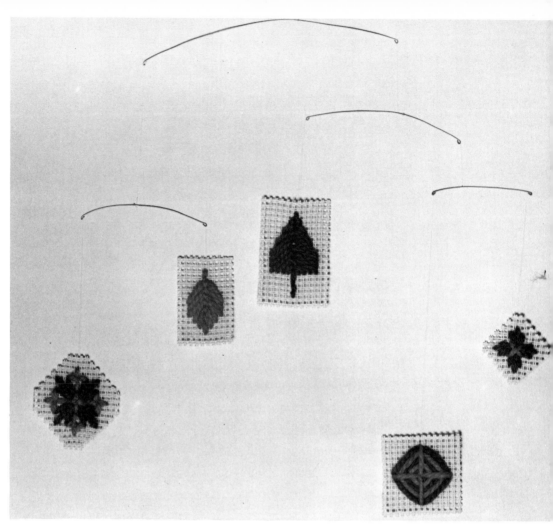

5 mesh rug canvas

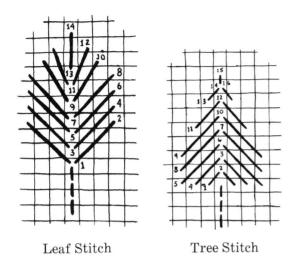

Leaf Stitch Tree Stitch

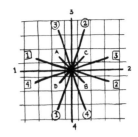

Work small cross stitch last. Fasten wool at center back before starting each new set of stitches.

around with white nail polish. Paint both pieces of the sets. Be sure to have the windows open while you are doing this, the nail polish smell is pretty strong.

When the pieces are dry, sew the sets together on the second row of mesh. Use white sewing thread or the transparent nylon. When all the sets are finished, wire cutting is the next step.

Cut one piece ten inches long. Cut another six inches long, one five inches long, and the last four inches. Stroke the wire with your fingers to straighten it, but leave it with a slight curve. Make a little loop on each end of each rod using the needlenose pliers.

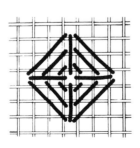

Point Russe stitch

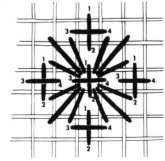

Triple Leviathan stitch

Lay all the rods out on a dark surface. Tie a long strand of thread from the center of the ten inch rod. Tie eighteen inch long strands of thread to the centers of all the short rods. Each one will ultimately be a different length, but the long length at first will give you plenty of room to adjust.

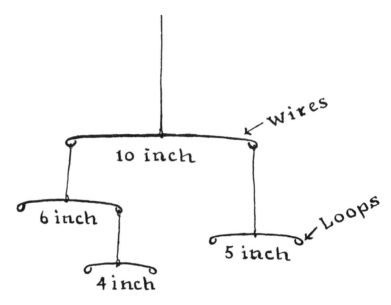

Tie the six inch rod to one end of the ten inch rod, tie the four inch rod to one end of the six inch rod. Tie the five inch rod from the other end of the ten inch rod.

Adjust the rod threads until you feel you have a graceful pattern. Now tie your needlepoint pieces on to the empty loops, having first tied an eighteen inch strand to the top of each one. Some of the pieces you will want to tie an inch from the rods, some as far away as ten inches. You should try to keep the pieces from hitting each other as they whirl in the air. A great deal of tieing and re-tieing may be necessary before you are satisfied.

Try to have someone help you when you hang the mobile up the first time. Otherwise the pieces are apt to go sliding along the rods into a tangle. When you have the rods in some sort of balance, put a drop of Elmer's glue on the thread knot on the rod. Hold it in place for a minute to let the glue dry. Now you are finished!

50 ¢

DATE DUE

AUG 13 '73	DEC 15'		
OCT 1 2			
OCT 2 9			
FEB 1 8			
MAR 2			
MAR 1 8			
MAY 14			
OCT 23'			
NOV 14'			
4/7			
AUG. 2			
OCT. 27			
SEP 8			
APR 1			
SEP 20'			

JUN 27